D1569058

Why you're my
FAVORITE TEACHER

Gift book for teachers
that totally make the grade

Thoughtful

Personalized

Unique

A book for my favorite teacher

____

From your student

____

< picture >

1

When I first met you
I thought to myself

2

The most important thing you taught me is

____

____

3

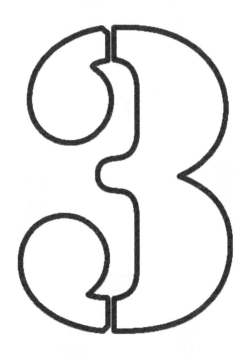

What I like about you most is

4

My favorite subject in your class is

____

____

5

3 words to describe your are

1. ______________________

2. ______________________

3. ______________________

6

You are really good at

____

____

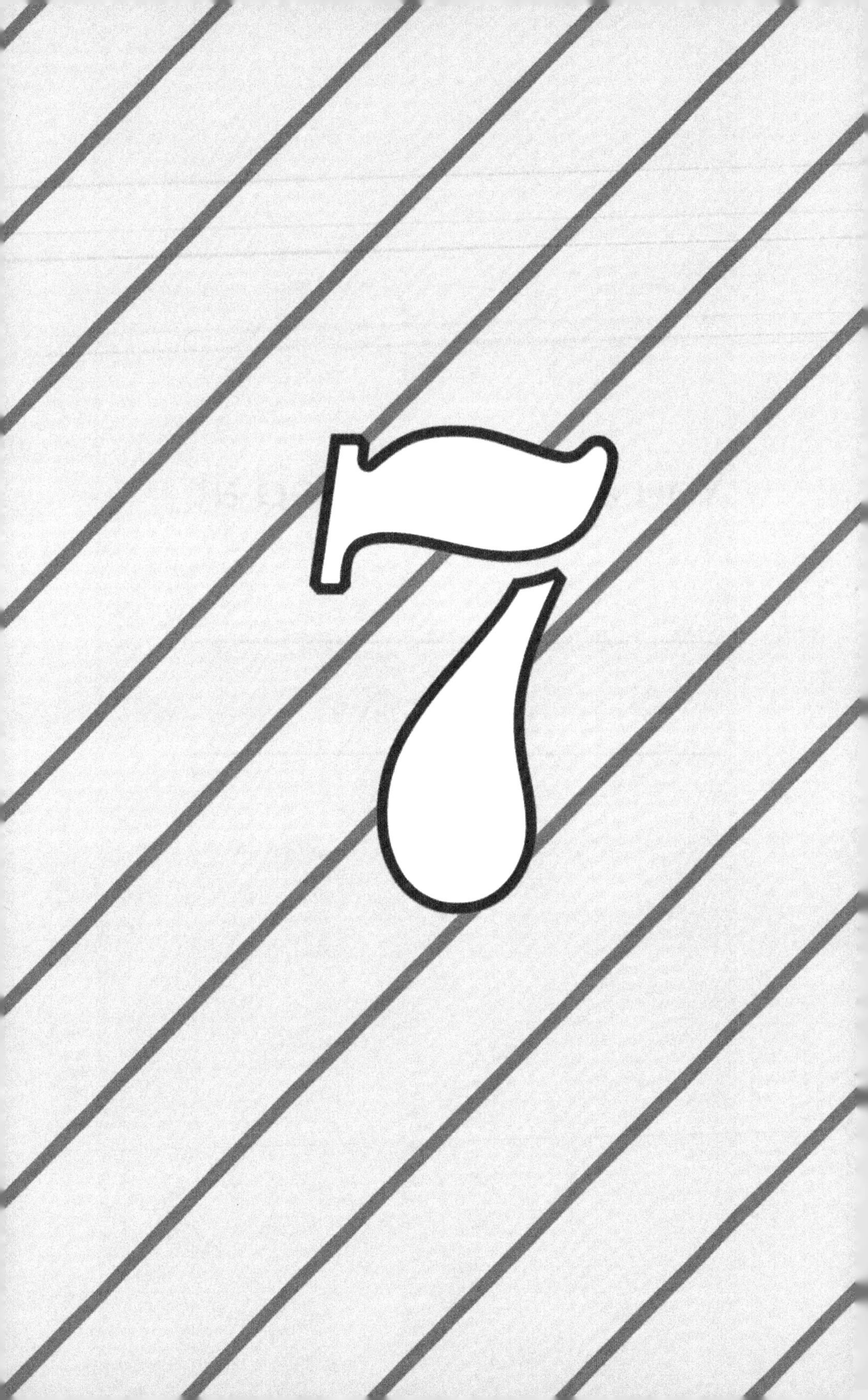
7

You would never

8

I like that you help me

____

____

9

You always say

10

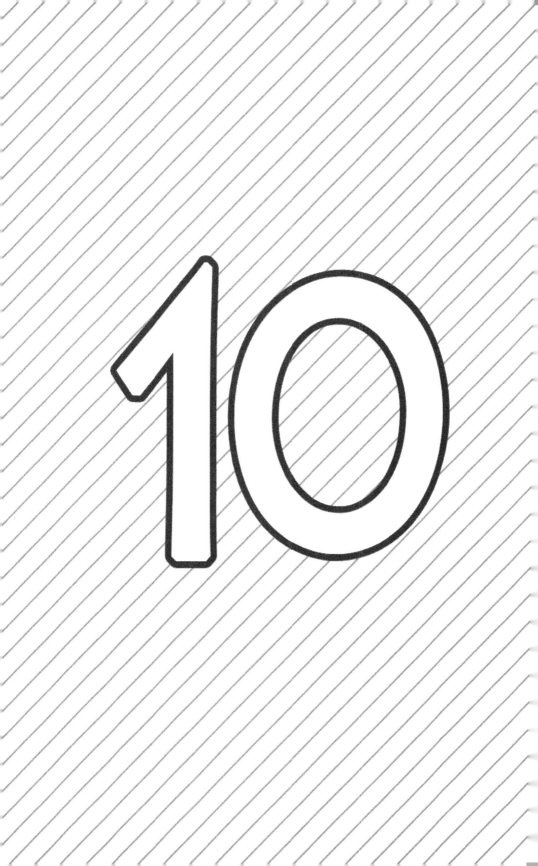

Another thing you like saying is

____

____

11

You make me feel

____

____

12

If you weren’t a teacher you’d be a great

13

My absolute favorite thing about you is

____

____

14

I'm thankful for you because

____

____

15

The best thing you did for our class this year is

____

____

16

When you're not my teacher anymore the thing I'll miss the most is

____

____

17

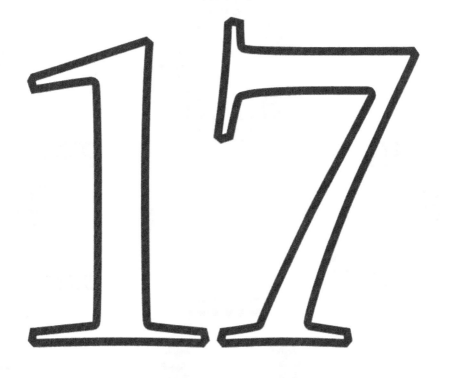

My favorite memory of you is

18

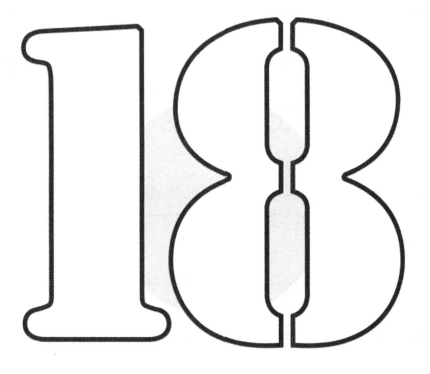

My favorite thing about school this year is

____

____

19

I think you're fun
because

20

I would like to thank you for

____

____

21

The best thing you do with our class is

____

____

22

You make me feel special when you

23

You make

____

more fun

24

My favorite thing I learned this year is

25

The silliest thing you said is

26

Your favorite sport is

27

You inspire your students to

28

Something I would like you to know is

29

The best advice
you've given me is

30

Your best character trait is

____

____

31

If you were a
superhero you'd be

32

You remind me of

33

I think the hardest part of your job is

____

____

34

My favorite class activity was

35

You find it really important that our class

36

When you're not at school you

37

I know you are
happy when you

____

____

38

If you could make a wish I think you'd wish for

____

____

39

Your favorite food is

____

____

40

During summer
break you go

41

If you could take us
on a field trip
anywhere, we'd go to

____

____

42

What I'll always remember of you is

43

I admire you for

44

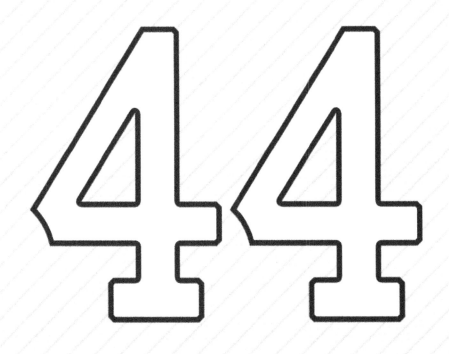

If you were an animal you'd be

45

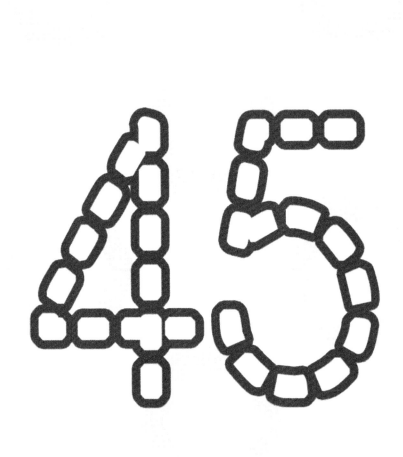

The coolest book I read this year is

46

Your favorite music is

47

I love that you are
really passionate
about

48

You get frustrated when our class

____

____

49

When you want to motivate me you say

____

____

50

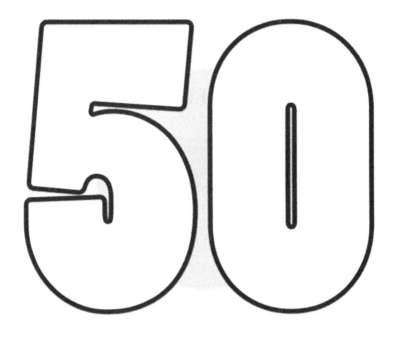

Your secret super hero power is

___

___

Made in the USA
Monee, IL
12 May 2022

96264411R20057